THE THIRD TESTAMENT

part I

THE GOD OF
DANIEL RELIGION 2016

DANIEL MCTAGGART

Order this book online at www.trafford.com
or email orders@trafford.com

Most Trafford titles are also available at major online book retailers.

Scripture quotations marked KJV are from the Holy Bible, King James Version
(Authorized Version). First published in 1611. Quoted from the KJV Classic
Reference Bible, Copyright © 1983 by The Zondervan Corporation.

Scripture quotations marked NJB are from The New Jerusalem Bible,
copyright © 1985 by Darton, Longman & Todd, Ltd. and Doubleday,
a division of Random House, Inc. Reprinted by Permission.

Print information available on the last page.

ISBN: 978-1-4907-6591-4 (hc)
ISBN: 978-1-4907-6592-1 (e)

Scripture quotations marked KJV are from the Holy Bible, King James Version
(Authorized Version). First published in 1611. Quoted from the KJV Classic
Reference Bible, Copyright © 1983 by The Zondervan Corporation.

Scripture quotations marked NJB are from The New Jerusalem Bible,
copyright © 1985 by Darton, Longman & Todd, Ltd. and Doubleday,
a division of Random House, Inc. Reprinted by Permission.

Trafford rev. 11/11/2016

www.trafford.com
North America & international
toll-free: 1 888 232 4444 (USA & Canada)
fax: 812 355 4082

July 1, 2015

Invitation to join the GOD of DANIEL RELIGION

Ladies and Gentlemen:

I am a former Iowa judge. After nearly 10 years I abruptly quit and turned to religion. Between November 1983 and January 1984 I read two and part of a third bible, concluding that my religion, Catholicism, was corrupt and I immediately dropped out.

During the next four years, I had no religion. I visited with Mormon missionaries from time to time and also with Jehovah's Witnesses once. The latter left a book, AID TO BIBLE UNDERSTANDING, by my door one day. It was very helpful as it listed biblical topics in alphabetical order.

I would estimate that it was 90% complete. I also had a bible study guide from the Oxford Press, but used AID much more. For some reason, not explained, the Witnesses came out with a 2-book *Insight into Scriptures*. I concluded that AID was a better resource.

In 1987 I finally mastered *Roe v. Wade,* the famous case on abortion. At the time I identified 17 major errors in the case. I also made a major discovery in interpreting Daniel 14 (found only in Catholic and Mormon Bibles): If one is truly a man of God he will be able to identify and expose false religion to the government. I hope to be that person.

At that time, I found the God of Daniel religion with one belief: that a religion must be in truth to be acceptable to God.

On December 7, 1997 I handwrote a letter of 17 pages extending the religion, based primarily on the Book of Matthew. When I tried to publish a summary of my religion to the world in a weekly shopper, my guardian – brother, had me placed in Faith Regional Health Services for evaluation for approximately three weeks; from there, about four months at Norfolk Regional Center. No staff person mentioned religion at either institution, as I recall.

Beginning in 2000 I began writing my own Bible study guide. I worked on it for 7 or 8 years, I now call it THE THIRD TESTAMENT, a collection of 43 books adding to the Bible. The text was not published and has been lost. I am satisfied that this comprehensive religion is an acceptable substitute.

A 13-page version of this was typed in 2012 with inmates at the Nebraska State Penitentiary as the primary audience.

I have always thought it a very daunting task for anyone to attempt to speak for God. Accordingly, I have adopted Quasi Quasi (as if, as if I speak for God).

I have decided that this work will speak for itself and I will do little or no speaking publicly on behalf of it.

The book is very biblically oriented, strongly adhering to the teachings of Jesus, except on one point.

Given that there exists thousands of religions ostensibly assuming to speak for Jesus, the obvious question is why one more? Jesus said: "On this rock I shall build my church." Since he didn't say churches I argue that only the God of Daniel religion qualifies as his church. I trust that I have proved it.

May 1, 2016

As I finished this work, I noticed that at places I added to old testament teachings in addition to Daniel 14 and interpreted several passages of Jesus as no one else past or present has done. Thus I now resurrect the title THE THIRD TESTAMENT part 1 as there should be proof somewhere that the words of Jesus are true. The God of Daniel 2016 is now a subtitle.

I submit that such proof was lacking only until recently; no one in the past has ever *proved* that a single utterance of Jesus was true. Many think so, many believe, but independent proof is lacking.

Inasmuch as I am designating this a biblical text, I am adding numbers to the extended verses.

1. I would agree that if my endeavor to present the beginning of an additional testament falls short, that someone somewhere will pick up the pieces and do it right.

> i.   Reader beware, this book is unprecedented, innovative, unique and bold.
>
> ii. Obviously, this is among the very briefest of books ever published, but intentionally so. The goal is to highlight in a few pages why I speak for God today and probably no one else does. Subsequent books will be more detailed.
>
> iii. I was surprised at the sales price the publisher set, but I consider this work an indispensable companion to the bible which contains much which is difficult to comprehend. I certainly have no objection to anyone checking it out at the library prior to making an ownership decision.

iv. As I state in a couple of places: Truth is where you find it. I found it after more than 30 years of pain staking research. It is my final thought that Jesus, the Father, and the Holy Spirit are happier today than last week.

v. Some years ago my cousin Kevin Martin said to me that religion is not important, Kevin doesn't talk a lot, at least not to me. He knew that I was anguished by my emersion in the subject. I took this as a challenge. I don't necessarily look for people that agree with me, but I'm always glad to be challenged about important matters. At the time I had no response for Kevin except for the fact that it was a very significant observation. Today I can respond to him: religion is important as long as it is the right one.

vi. Consider the following words of Jesus:

[Mathew 7:7-8]

7 Ask and it shall be given you; seek, and ye shall find: knock, and it shall be opened unto you:

8 For every one that asketh receiveth; and he that seeketh findeth; and to him that knocketh it shall be opened.

2. I have "askethed" and "seekethed" and I have found much over the years. There is more to ask and more to seek. I trust that I am knocking on heaven's door.

I

INTRODUCTION

The Beatitudes

I prefer THE NEW JERUSALEM version over others because the text features "happy" rather than "blessed."

2. How happy are the poor in spirit;

theirs in the kingdom of heaven.

Happy the gentle,
they shall have the earth for their heritage.

Happy those who mourn;
they shall be comforted.

Happy those who hunger and thirst for what is right:
they shall be satisfied.

Happy the merciful;
they shall have mercy shown them.

Happy the pure in heart:

they shall see God.

Happy the peacemakers:
they shall be called sons of God.

Happy those who are persecuted in the cause of right;
theirs is the kingdom of heaven.

Philosophy

3.   [Ecclesiastes 3:1-8]

[1] To every *thing* there is a season, and a time to every purpose under the heaven:
[2] A time to be born, and a time to die; a time to plant, and a time to pluck up that which is planted:
[3] A time to kill, and a time to heal; a time to break down, and a time to build up;
[4] A time to weep, and a time to laugh; a time to mourn, and a time to dance;
[5] A time to cast away stones, and a time to gather stones together; a time to embrace, and a time to refrain from embracing;
[6] A time to get, and a time to lose; a time to keep, and a time to cast away;
[7] A time to rend, and a time to sew; a time to keep silence, and a time to speak;
[8] A time to love, and a time to hate; a time of war, and a time of peace.

4.   These words from Ecclesiastes give me hope and inspiration. The message to me is that even if something has gone on for years, perhaps centuries, the opposite is bound to come about.

5. In my view this passage is the highlight of the Old Testament. As of this writing the world appears to be in chaos. But I am certain that God has all in hand. Read on:

6. [Ecclesiastes 3:9-17]

⁹ What profit hath he that worketh in that wherein he laboreth?

¹⁰ I have seen the travail, which God hath given to the sons of men to be exercised in it.

¹¹ He hath made every *thing* beautiful in his time: also he hath set the world in their heart, so that no man can find out the work that God maketh from the beginning to the end.

¹² I know that *there is* no good in them, but for a *man* to rejoice, and do good in his life.

¹³ And also that every man should eat and drink, and enjoy the good of all his labour, it *is* the gift of God.

¹⁴ I know that, whatsoever God doeth it shall be for ever: nothing can be put to it, nor any thing taken from it: and God doeth *it*, that *men* should fear before him.

¹⁵ That which hath been is now; and that which is to be hath already been; and God requireth that which is past.

¹⁶ And moreover I saw under the sun the place of judgment, that wickedness was there; and the place of righteousness, that iniquity was there.

¹⁷ I said in mine heart, God shall judge the righteous and the wicked: for *there* is a time there for every purpose and for every work.

II

God is eternal, All-truthful, All happy
Almighty, All-knowing, All-wise,
All-just, Good, Perfect,
One, The Creator.

2. There are three persons in one God. Father, Son, and Holy Spirit, but if you don't believe this I don't think you'll be condemned.

3. Jesus is the Son of God and he said: "I am the Way, the Truth and the Life; no one comes to the Father except through me." John 14:6 No other religious leader has made such a bold statement. With these words of Jesus, it is difficult to envision what more could or should be added. The words of Paul may be suspect. If Jesus wanted 13 apostles, he certainly could have appointed that many; the chapter called Acts of the Apostles chronicles the life and times of Paul over several years, mentioning little to nothing about the original 12.

4. Jesus died to redeem our sins and he rose from the dead.

Luke 24:1–8.

[1] Now upon the first day of the week, very early in the morning, they came unto the sepulcher, bringing the spices which they had prepared, and certain others with them.

² And they found the stone rolled away from the sepulchre.

³ And they entered in, and found not the body of the Lord Jesus.

⁴ And it came to pass, as they were much perplexed thereabout, behold, two men stood by them in shining garments:

⁵ And as they were afraid, and bowed down *their* faces to the earth, they said unto them, why seek ye the living among the dead?

⁶ He is not here, but is risen: remember how he spake unto you when he was yet in Galilee,

⁷ Saying, the Son of man must be delivered into the hands of sinful men, and be crucified, and the third day rise again.

⁸ They remembered his words.

5. There will be a second coming. Only God the Father knows when that will be. Luke 21:25-28

[Luke 21:25-28]

²⁵ And there shall be signs in the sun, and in the moon, and in the stars; and upon the earth distress of nations, with perplexity; the sea and the waves roaring;

²⁶ Men's hearts failing them for fear, and for looking after those things which are coming on the earth: for the powers of heaven shall be shaken.

²⁷ And then shall they see the Son of man coming in a cloud with power and great glory.

²⁸ And when these things begin to come to pass, then look up, and lift up your heads; for your redemption draweth nigh.

6. God is a sexual being. Jesus was created before the creation of earth. There is no report or evidence that a God of mother was involved in this first creation, so the only reasonable, logical conclusion is that Jesus was formed by a (homo) sexual act of God the Father.

7. **The Ten Commandments**

[Exodus 20:1-17]

[1] And God spake all these words, saying,

[2] I *am* the Lord thy God, which have brought thee out of the land of Egypt, out of the house of bondage.

[3] Thou shalt have no other gods before me.

[4] Thou shalt not make unto thee any graven image, or any likeness of any thing that is in heaven above, or in the water under the earth:

[5] Thou shalt not bow down thyself to them, nor serve them: for I the Lord thy God *am* a jealous God, visiting the iniquity of the fathers upon the children unto the third and fourth generation of them that hate me;

[6] And shewing mercy unto thousands of them that love me, and keep my commmandments.

[7] Thou shalt not take the name of the Lord thy God in vain; for the Lord will not hold him guiltless that taketh his name in vain.

[8] Remember the Sabbath day, to keep it holy.

[9] Six days shalt thou labour, and do all thy work:

[10] But the seventh day *is* the Sabbath of the the Lord thy God; in it thou shalt not do any work, thou, nor thy son, nor thy daughter, thy manservant, nor thy maidservant, nor thy cattle, nor thy stranger that is within thy gates:

¹¹ For in six days the Lord made heaven and earth, the sea, and all that in them is, and rested the seventh day: wherefore the Lord blessed the Sabbath day, and hallowed it.

¹² Honour thy father and thy mother: that thy days may be long upon the land which the Lord thy God giveth thee.

¹³ Thou shalt not kill.

¹⁴ Thou shalt not commit adultery.

¹⁵ Thou shalt not steal.

¹⁶ Thou shalt not bear false witness against thy neighbour.

¹⁷ Thou shalt not covet thy neighbour's house, thou shalt not covet thy neighbour's wife, nor his man servant, nor his maidservant, nor his ox, nor his ass, nor any *thing* that is thy neighbour's.

8. The following are some general principles.

    a) Secret prayer at all times. Matthew 6:5-16
    b) Secret alms at all times Matthew 6:1-4
    c) Loan without expectation of being paid. Luke 6:34
    d) Do unto others as you would have them do to you Matthew 7:12
    e) Truth is the Word of God, as defined by Jesus.
    f) The testimony of two witnesses is true.
        This is the only yardstick or principle of ascertaining truth from falsehood or fiction. If a saying is attributed to Jesus, it is true only if confirmed by two sources. *Possible* sources are the 4 gospels and the rest of the New Testament. A source need not be an eyewitness. I am claiming to be the ultimate source (God's doing not mine; I believe he programmed me to search for the truth).
    g) The truth shall set you free. Jesus didn't say freedom from what or in what sense? I believe that it is my responsibility to explore this point – but not right now.

III

Jesus announced a number of other principles to guide our behavior. Below are what I deem to be the most important.

2. Keep the ten commandments. See Exodus 20:1-17 in previous chapter. Surprisingly emphasis is on not to defraud and not on a prohibition of murder. See [Mark 10:19].

19 Thou knowest the commandments, do not commit adultery, do not kill, do not steal, do not bear false witness, defraud not, honour they father and mother.

The Greatest Commandment:

[Luke 10:25-28]

25 And, behold, a certain lawyer stood up, and tempted him, saying, Master, what shall I do to inherit eternal life?
26 He said unto him, what is written in the law? How readest thou?
27 And he answering said, thou shalt love the Lord thy God with all thy heart, and with all thy soul, and with all thy strength, and with all thy mind; and thy neighbor as thyself.
28 And he said unto him, thou hast answered right: this do, and thou shalt live.

3. Their entire being? I'm claiming to be closer to God than anyone in the world at this time. I'm on the verge of loving him wholeheartedly. I'll explain whole heartedly, which does not mean a "good Christian," because a good Christian is under the influence of Paul and doesn't know that not everything in the gospels are true.

> Comment: How many people love God with their entire being? As explained above, it is insufficient to be "a good Christian."

4. Secrecy

a) Alms

[Matthew 6:1-4]

¹ Take heed that ye do not your alms before men, to be seen of them: otherwise ye have no reward of your Father which is in heaven.

² Therefore when thou doest *thine* alms, do not sound a trumpet before thee, as the hypocrites do in the synagogues and in the streets, that they may have glory of men. Verily I say unto you, they have their reward.

³ But when thou doest alms, let not thy left hand know what thy right hand doeth:

⁴ That thine alms may be in secret: and thy Father which seeth in secret himself shall reward thee openly.

> Comment: Jesus' words are clear: give alms in private. I don't see how God could be pleased with the many benefits and fundraisers that go on in this country. These practices must stop immediately.

b) Praying

Comment: The word is prayed in private. I would never pray
in a church or community breakfast – not even at
meal time with family and friends.

Church services should consist of readings from the
Old Testament and the gospels. I can think of no
one qualified to give a homily.

It is of great consternation that the pro-life
community rebukes Jesus at all times by their
prayers in public. Jesus provided the perfect prayer.
The Lord's prayer. He also approved the publican's
prayer. "God, be merciful to me a sinner." Luke
18:14

c) Forgiveness

[Matthew 6:15]

15 But if ye forgive not men their trespasses, neither will
your father forgive your trespasses.

Comment: Jesus couldn't have been any clearer

d) Fasting

[Matthew 6:18]

18 That thou appear not unto men to fast, but unto thy
Father which is in secret: and thy Father, which seeth in
secret, shall reward thee openly.

Comment: If the Catholics choose to fast in their way on Ash Wednesday and Fridays instead it is difficult to envision that they followed Jesus.

5. Generosity

   a) Loaning

[Matthew 5:42]

⁴² Give to him that asketh thee, and from him that would borrow of thee turn not thou away.

[Luke 6:32-36]

³² For if ye love them which love you, what thank have ye? For sinners also love those that love them.
³³ And if ye do good to them which do good to you, what thank have ye? For sinners also do even the same.
³⁴ And if ye lend to them of whom ye hope to receive, what thank have ye? For sinners also lend to sinners, to receive as much again.
³⁵ But love ye your enemies, and do good, and lend hoping for nothing again; and your reward shall be great, and ye shall be the children of the Highest: for he is kind unto the unthankful and to the evil.
³⁶ Be ye therefore merciful, as your Father also is merciful.

[Luke 6:38]

³⁸ Give and it shall be given unto you; good measure, pressed down, and shaken together, and running over, shall men give into your bosom. For with the same measure that ye mete withal it shall be measured to you again.

> *Comment*: This is a rather novel principle, but since Jesus said so, it must be right.

b) The less fortunate

[Matthew 25:31-46]

[31] When the Son of man shall come in his glory, and all the holy angels with him, then shall he sit upon the throne of his glory:

[32] And before him shall be gathered all nations: and he shall separate them one from another, as a shepherd divideth his sheep from the goats:

[33] And he shall set the sheep on his right hand, but the goats on the left.

[34] Then shall the King say unto them on his right hand, come, ye blessed of my Father, inherit the kingdom prepared for you from the foundation of the world:

[35] For I was an hungered, and ye gave me meat: I was thirsty, and ye gave me drink: I was a stranger, and ye took me in:

[36] Naked, and ye clothed me: I was sick, and ye visited me: I was in prison, and ye came unto me.

[37] Then shall the righteous answer him, saying, Lord, when saw we thee an hungred, and fed *thee*? Or thirsty, and gave *thee* drink?

[38] When saw we *thee* a stranger, and took thee in? Or naked, and clothed *thee*?

[39] Or when saw we thee sick, or in prison, and came unto thee?

[40] And the King shall answer and say unto them, verily I say unto you, inasmuch as ye have done it unto one of the least of these my brethren, ye have done it unto me.

⁴¹ Then shall he say also unto them on the left hand, depart from me, ye cursed, into everlasting fire, prepared for the devil and his angels:

⁴² For I was an hungred, and ye gave me no meat: I was thirsty, and ye gave me no drink:

⁴³ I was a stranger, and ye took me not in: naked, and ye clothed me not: sick, and in prison, and ye visited me not.

⁴⁴ Then shall they also answer him, saying, Lord, when saw we thee an hungred, or athirst, or a stranger, or naked, or sick, or in prison, and did not minister unto thee?

⁴⁵ Then shall he answer them, saying, verily I say unto you, inasmuch as ye did it not to one of the least of these, ye did it not to me.

⁴⁶ And these shall go away into everlasting punishment: but the reighteous into life eternal.

Comment: I don't think that this requirement is met by donating to a food party or soup kitchen. I don't think you are clothing the naked by giving unwanted clothing to a thrift shop.

c)   Riches

[Matthew 6:24]

²⁴ No man can serve two masters: for either he will hate the one, and love the other; or else he will hold to the one, and despise the other. Ye cannot serve God and the mammon.

[Luke 19:1-10]

¹ And Jesus entered and passed through Jericho.

² And, behold, *there* was a man named Zac-chae'us, which was the chief among the publicans, and he was rich.

³ And he sought to see Jesus who he was; and could not for the press, because he was little of stature.

⁴ And he ran before, and climbed up into a sycamore tree to see him: for he was to pass that way.

⁵ And when Jesus came to the place, he looked up, and saw him, and said unto him, Zac-chae'us make haste, and come down; for today I must abide at thy house.

⁶ And he made haste, and came came down, and received him joyfully.

⁷ And when they saw *it*, they all murmered saying, that he was gone to be guest with a man that is a sinner.

⁸ And Zac-chae'us stood, and said unto the Lord; Behold, Lord, the half of my goods I give to the poor; and if I have taken any thing from any man by false accusation, I restore *him* fourfold.

⁹ And Jesus said unto him, this day is salvation come to this house, forsomuch as he also is a son of Abraham.

¹⁰ For the Son of man is come to seek and to save that which was lost.

Comment: Many people want to be rich. The key is to give the riches away, or a substantial amount. This may be what it means to be poor in spirit. I've never been rich. I was middle class the first 40 years or so and poor the last 3 decades. My sole income since 1969 has been social security. I hope I'm not complaining. The only real hardship is funding my publishing ventures. And an unfulfilled dream is to return to lakeside living.

Had I been rich, I don't think I would have had the time or inclination to found this religion. The religion was formed gradually, in spurts. I have taken many tentative positions which have been discarded over time.

d) Treasures

[Matthew 6:19-21]

[19] Lay not up for yourselves treasures upon earth, where moth and rust doth corrupt, and where thieves break through and steal:

[20] But lay up for yourselves treasures in heaven, where neither moth nor rust doth corrupt, and where thieves do not break through nor steal:

[21] For where your treasure is, there will your heart be also.

Comment: As I interpret this passage I think possessions could be substituted for treasures. The concept is closely akin to riches, I believe.

6. Personal Relationships

a) Don't judge

[Matthew 7:1-2]

[1] Judge not, that ye be not judged.

[2] For with what judgment ye judge, ye shall be judged: and with what measure ye mete, it shall be measured to you again.

Comment: At one juncture, I thought this meant that the occupation as judge, which I held, was prohibited, but now I believe that person-to-person, we shouldn't judge others.

b) Love enemies

[Matthew 5:43-48]

[43] Ye have heard that it hath been said, thou shalt love thy neighbour, and hate thine enemy.

[44] But I say unto you, love your enemies, bless them that curse you, do good to them that hate you, and pray for them which despitefully use you, and persecute you;

[45] That ye may be the children of your Father which is in heaven: for he maketh his sun to rise on the evil and on the good, and sendeth rain on the just and on the unjust.

[46] For if ye love them which love you, what reward have ye? Do not even the publicans the same?

[47] And if ye salute your brethren only, what do ye more than others? Do not even the publicans so?

[48] Be ye therefore perfect, even as your Father which is in heaven is perfect.

Comment: As of today there is no one I hate, but as this is sure to be a radical, unpopular document, I'm sure I'll have many enemies.

c) Eating with sinners

[Luke 5:29-32]

[29] And Levi made him a great feast in his own house: and there was a great company of publicans and of others that sat down with them.

³⁰ But their scribes and Pharisees murmered against his disciples, saying, what do ye eat and drink with publicans and sinners?

³¹ And Jesus answering said unto them, they that are whole need not a physician: but they that are sick.

³² I came not to call the righteous, but sinners to repentance.

Comment: I am not picky with whom I eat.

7.   Family considerations

    a)   My mother

Comment   I remember my mother repeating that I get to heaven. Did your parents instruct you similarly? She told me she never read the bible. Many friends and relatives often called her a saint.

    b)   Little children

Comment   Mother repeating that all that is important is that her 9 children get to heaven

[Matthew 19:13-15]

¹³ Then were there brought unto him little children, that he should put his hands on them, and pray: and the disciples rebuked them.

¹⁴ But Jesus said, suffer little children, and forbid them not, to come unto me: for of such is the kingdom of heaven.

¹⁵ And he laid his hands on them, and departed thence.

[Matthew 11:25]

[25] At that time Jesus answered and said, I thank thee, O Father, Lord of heaven and earth, because thou hast hid these things from the wise and prudent, and hast revealed them unto babes.

[Mark 10:13-18]

[13] And they brought young children to him, that he should touch them: and *his* disciples rebuked those that brought *them*.

[14] But when Jesus saw it, he was much displeased, and said unto them, suffer the little children to come unto me, and forbid them not: for of such is the kingdom of God.

[15] Verily I say unto you, whosoever shall not receive the kingdom of God as a little child, he shall not enter therein.

[16] And he took them up in his arms, put his hands upon them, and blessed them.

[17] And when he was gone forth into the way, there came one running, and kneeled to him, and asked him, Good Master, what shall I do that I may inherit eternal life?

[18] And Jesus said unto him, why callest thou me good? There is none good but one, *that* is, God.

Comment: Though the points made are simple, the classifications are astounding. I think it means that we are to have the faith that small children have of their parents. On average it may be that the highly educated will have more difficulty in grasping Jesus' principles than the relatively uneducated (Please note that I've had 4 years or college and 3 of law school).

c) All children

[Matthew 7:9-11]

⁹ Or what man is there of you, whom if his son ask bread, will he give him a stone?

¹⁰ Or if he ask a fish, will he give him a serpent?

¹¹ If ye then, being evil, know how to give good gifts unto your children, how much more shall your Father which is in heaven give good things to them that ask him?

Comment: Then only a child abuser would disagree.

8. Conclusions

a) Believing and acting

[John 3:16-21]

¹⁶ For God so loved the world, that he gave his only begotten Son, that whosoever believeth in him should not perish, but have everlasting life.

¹⁷ For God sent not his Son into the world to condemn the world; but that the world through him might be saved.

¹⁸ He that believeth on him is not condemned: but he that believeth not in condemned already, because he hath not believed in the name of the only begotten Son of God.

¹⁹ And this is the condemnation, that light is come into the world, and men loved darkness rather than light, because their deeds were evil.

²⁰ For every one that doeth evil hateth the light, neither cometh to the light, lest his deeds should be reproved.

²¹ But he that doeth truth cometh to the light, that his deeds may be made manifest, that they are wrought in God.

Comment: John 3:16 is the most commonly cited and quoted verse in the bible, I think. It is not sufficient to say "I believe." One must, as stated below, take action. One must be born again. *Id.*, 3:4-5, 7.

b) The will of the father

[Matthew 7:21-23]

²¹ Not every one that saith unto me, Lord, Lord, shall enter into the kingdom of heaven; but he that doeth the will of my Father which is in heaven.

²² Many will say to me in that day, Lord, Lord, have we not prophesied in thy name? And in thy name have cast out devils? And in thy name done many wonderful works?

²³ And then will I profess unto them, I never knew you: depart from me, ye that work iniquity.

Comment: Jesus is speaking for the Father and is acting on behalf of the Father.

[John 5:19-24]

¹⁹ Then answered Jesus and said unto them, verily, verily, I say unto you, The Son can do nothing of himself, but what he seeth the Father do: for what things soever he doeth, these also doeth the Son likewise.

²⁰ For the Father loveth the Son, and sheweth him all things that himself doeth: and he will shew him greater works than these, that ye may marvel.

²¹ For as the Father raiseth up the dead, and quickeneth *them*; even so the Son quickeneth whom he will.

²² For the Father judgeth no man, but hath committed all judgment unto the Son:

²³ That all men should honour the Son, even as they honour the Father. He that honoureth not the Son honoureth not the Father which hath sent him.

²⁴ Verily, verily, I say unto you, he that heareth my word, and believeth on him that sent me, hath everlasting life, and shall not come into condemnation; but is passed from death unto life.

c)   Building on a strong foundation

[Matthew 7:24-27]

²⁴ Therefore whosoever heareth these sayings of mine, and doeth them, I will liken him unto a wise man, which built his house upon a rock:

²⁵ And the rain descended, and the floods came, and the winds blew, and beat upon that house; and it fell not: for it was founded upon a rock.

²⁶ And every one that heareth these sayings of mine, and doeth them not, shall be likened unto a foolish man, which built his house upon the sand.

²⁷ And the rain descended, and the floods came, and the winds blew, and beat upon that house; and it fell: and great was the fall of it.

Comment: Those hearing Jesus' words and acting on them is indeed acting wisely that's why John 3:16 by itself is not enough.

d)   There is a direct correlation between truth and light.

[John 3:20-21]

[20] For every one that doeth evil hateth the light, neither cometh to the light, lest his deeds should be reproved.

[21] But he that doeth truth cometh to the light, that his deeds may be made manifest, that they are wrought in God.

Comment: We have been in darkness since Jesus left the earth. He promises that if we do what is true, we will be in the light. I suggest that no one has been in the light or in truth since Jesus left the earth.

e)   Perfection is a goal

[Matthew 5:48]

[48] Be ye therefore perfect, even as your Father which is in heaven is perfect.

Comment: It is often stated that "no one is perfect" this has probably been true so far. As suggested above, if in truth they will be in light.

f)   The truth will make one free

[John 8:31-38]

[31] Then said Jesus to those Jews which believed on him, if ye continue in my word, *then* are ye my disciples indeed;

[32] And ye shall know the truth, and the truth shall make you free.

[33] They answered him, we be Abraham's seed, and were never in bondage to any man: how sayest thou, ye shall be made free?

[34] Jesus answered them, verily, verily, I say unto you, whosoever committeth sin is the servant of sin.

³⁵ And the servant abideth not in the house for ever: *but* the Son abideth ever.

³⁶ If the Son therefore shall make you free, ye shall be free indeed.

³⁷ I know that ye are Abraham's seed; but ye seek to kill me, because my word hath no place in you.

³⁸ I speak that which I have seen with my Father: and ye do that which ye have seen with your father.

Comment: Verses 31 and 32 make for a very powerful message. It is the word of God that shall set us free. Freedom from what? I would suggest sin and death.

g) Jesus stated that there is only one sin that will not be forgiven, the sin of blasphemy against the spirit.

Comment: I interpret spirit as the truth, the Word of God.

IV

Man is made in God's image and likeness.

[Genesis 1:26]

²⁶ And God said, let us make man in our image, after our likeness: and let them have dominion over the fish of the sea, and over the fowl of the air, and over the cattle, and over all the earth, and over every creeping thing that creepeth upon the earth.

[Genesis 2:18]

¹⁸ And the Lord God said, it is not good that the man should be alone; I will make him an help meet for him.

[Genesis 2:20]

²⁰ And Adam gave names to all cattle, and to the fowl of the air, and to every beast of the field; but for Adam there was not found an help meet for him.

Thus in seeking a help meet for man, God first considered cattle, fowl and beasts. The creation of woman was afterthought according to chapter 2.

[Genesis 2:21-23]

²¹ And the Lord God caused a deep sleep to fall upon Adam, and he slept: and he took one of his ribs, and closed up the flesh instead thereof;

²² And the rib, which the Lord God had taken from man, made he a woman, and brought her unto the man.

²³ And Adam said, this is now bone of my bones, and flesh of my flesh: she shall be called Woman, because she was taken out of man.

Based upon the above passages it is logical to believe that God considers man superior to woman.

2. "Christians" seem to cling to an unarticulated view that sexual relations are only for the married. The God of Daniel religion holds to the position that the Bible is the source and exclusive guide to all matters relating to sexuality.

    a) Man and woman

        Heterosexuality is the norm for most males
        Two shall be as one flesh
        [Genesis 2:24]

²⁴ Therefore shall a man leave his father and his mother, and shall cleave unto his wife: and they shall be one flesh.

3. Rape in old testament times was not a criminal offense, but a matter between a man and woman. If he committed rape he should be made to marry the woman. If this didn't happen, he was required to pay her father a sum of money. See generally, Ben Edward Ackerley, *The X-Rated Bible* (Federal House March 1, 1999).

4. Fornication is forbidden. Matthew 5:17, 32. While sexual activity gives pleasure to both individuals, I sense from the Bible that the primary function of the (married) woman was to give birth to children.

And of course, adultery was forbidden in the 10 commandments.

b)   Man on man

Sodomy is forbidden in the Old Testament.

[Leviticus 20:13]

[13] If a man also lie with mankind, as he lieth with a woman, both of them have committed an abomination: they shall surely be put to death; their blood shall be upon them.

5.   Does it prohibit other man-to-man sexual activities? I think it is a fair statement that most adults are sexual human beings. I think it is also a fair statement that God made a minority of men to be sexually attracted to other men.

6.   I begin by noting what is not denounced in the Bible: a man masturbating himself. If he can do so, can he also ask or allow a friend to do the same thing with his hand? I am sure that this could be accomplished whether or not the two "lieth" together. I submit that the Old Testament is too lacking on detail to forbid masturbation by another. If we go on to oral sex, I am unable to conclude that man-to-man can not so partake.

7.   Finally, some men are bisexual, both hetero-and homosexual.

c)   Woman on woman

8. Biblically speaking, sexuality is a guy thing. This will explain why rape was not considered so serious.

9. A woman being sexually involved with another woman is not mentioned in the Bible. As a male on the outside, I think it silly but more power to them.

10. Why is sodomy an abomination? Since the Bible failed to state why, I can only speculate that the mixture between one's sperm and another man's fecal material may be reprehensible to God. I can fathom no other reason.

11. Health officials urge a man to wear a condom if he is going to sodomize a mate as this is likely to prevent the development of HIV which may lead to AIDS. I have no idea of how many men so involved practice safe sex in this regard.

12. If an unmarried man and a woman copulate and he's wearing a condom, the chances of a pregnancy are greatly diminished, of course.

13. Consequently, science has changed the physicalities surrounding sexual activities, so it is very arguable that protected sodomy and fornication are not risky – even morally.

14. Generally speaking, American society pays little attention to the Bible with regard to sexuality.

15. Rape is a serious crime in every state.

16. Legislators have classified crimes as sexual abuse in the first, second and third degrees, defining outlawing acts not prohibited in the Bible.

17. Fornication is recognized as a fundamental constitutional right according to the United States Supreme Court.

18. Sodomy is a fourteenth amendment liberty.

19. Same-sex marriage, commonly referred to as gay marriage has been given judicial approval throughout the United States.

20. Society, in the guise of protecting some unidentified harm, holds that minors don't have the right to participate in sexual activities with adults. A girl reaches puberty as young as 10, a boy at 12 —— when they are sexually adults.

21. In most states youth may engage in sex consensually with other youth without fear of prosecution. But there are harsh penalties for adult–minor sexual conduct.

22. The Bible sets no rules, regulations, guidelines or prohibitions with regard to child sexuality. In criminal prosecutions it would be arguable that defendants and their attorneys may rely on the Bible. Seemingly consensual sex between a 21-yr-old and a 15-yr-old is no different than two fifteen-year-olds going at it. Who does one trust: God or the government? Of course, if the child suffered specific, identifiable harm, the loving arms of the law would be appropriate.

23. I haven't seen the first amendment bible defense urged in any criminal use.

24. The Catholic Church has poured out millions and millions of dollars in many dioceses resulting in some instances in bankruptcy to compensate for priestly "sexual abuse," followed by hierarchical cover-ups. Most media accounts don't reveal the nature of the "abuses" but I suspect very few are founded on sodomy. Thus, I would raise the speculation that the Catholic Church in

America – and many parts of the world – may be fools for failing to read and understand the Bible.

25. Liberal abortion policies are theoretically consistent with the Bible. When Job was overtly miserable over a lengthy period of time, he regretted that he was not still-born which would have prevented a life of suffering. THE JERUSALEM BIBLE seems to extend this to the unborn. One aborted automatically goes to heaven. See Matthew 7:24-27 *Quoted on page 16 supra.*

26. I don't think that anyone in America would have "standing" to assert rights to protect the unborn's soul by requesting an abortion. Nor could any court act to save a soul. These matters are more thoroughly discussed in *ROE v. WADE* is Unconstitutional as Justice Blackmun Lied, written by yours truly and to be published hopefully in late December 2016.

27. The exact length of Job's misery was not reported in the biblical account. The book features him debating 3 friends, he was puzzled as to why he suffered so much, and the friends contending that it was because he sinned.

28. The book showed that he was the most upright man in the Old Testament. God finally appeared and told him that now was not the time to address his concerns, but praised him for being true to God. The result was a rich and rewarding extended life for Job.

29. If the greatest human in history continuously expressed to wish for God to end his suffering by taking his life, it logically follows that suicide is a viable option today for anyone who suffers much, concluding that life is no longer worth living.

30. There are many terminally ill patients in the United States enduring excruciating pain. If they choose to end their life, I don't

believe it is any of society's business. A sprinkling of states allow for assisted-suicide.

31. Courts have been involved with the issue, first Dr. Kevorkian was unable to establish a constitutional right in Michigan.

32. In 1997 the United States Supreme Court rejected the claim of constitutional right for physician-assisted suicide, citing a lack of precedent and a dispute among various unnamed "experts."

33. In reading these cases there is no evidence that any of the parties put forth the Book of Job as a controlling Biblical source. I truly believe that the issue will resurface and that Job will rule the day.

34. Job wasn't in imminent danger of death so the right to suicide exists even if death is not near.

35. This matter is discussed in the abortion book, mentioned above.

36. The God of Daniel Religion recognizes several rights of prisoners, which is guaranteed to raise eyebrows.

> a) to engage in consensual homosexual acts
> b) the right to possess and view pornography
> c) to smoke marijuana at government expense
> d) to smoke tobacco at government expense
> e) to consume alcohol at government expense
> f) to have good, nutritious food
> g) to have music up to 24 hours per day
> h) to have liberal visitation

37. All citizens have the above rights and in addition one that is guaranteed to be cloaked in controversy.

i) The right to a minimum wage of $20 per hour with employers exceeding employees numbering 50 to kick in $5 per employee to a fund for employers with less than 50 employees to draw from. Details will have to be worked out.

Comments

a) Sodomy is a liberty protected under the 14th Amendment *Lawrence v. Texas* (2003). All other sexual acts of a voluntary nature between men are constitutionally protected in that they involve freedom of association. And when they are so engaged they are pursuing happiness, an inalienable and self-evident right which must be protected by the government (the prison system) according to the Declaration of Independence.

I am quite sure that all prison systems have strict rules against voluntary sexual activity involving inmates, but these pre-date *Lawrence* and its progeny. I am also quite sure that it would be inconvenient for a prison to suddenly adopt a system in which sexual activity became commonplace.

If a prison can demonstrate a "legitimate" interest in prohibiting such activity in court its longstanding policy may prevail. However, if the only reason the policy exists is because someone a long time ago thought it a sound policy and every other prison system was doing the same provides an insufficient basis for demonstrating legitimacy.

Never having experimented with allowing inmates liberal sex, a prison is hardly in a position to argue persuasively all the institution of such a policy might be advantageous.

Finally, the God of Daniel religion establishes a first amendment right of all men in the world – including the prisons of course, to engage in homosexual acts. A practice should not be discouraged by a worker merely because it is deemed offensive to himself or corrections officers.

b) It may come as a shock to many people, but nowhere in the Bible is pornography prohibited. The Supreme Court seems to have accepted the possession and use of adult pornography as a protected activity, child pornography is entitled to no such protection. Since not frowned on by the Bible, the God of Daniel Religion holds that neither form of pornography is prohibited by God. As Job said, "Naked was I born..." I have no reason to believe that God is offended by the naked body, or photo thereof, adult or child.

c) In BUCKING POWER, to be published by Trafford Publishing in 2016, I present solid arguments for a constitutional right to possess and use marijuana as one aspect of the pursuit of happiness.

With the publication of this book, it also becomes an aspect of freedom of religion. The burden would be heavy on a prison system to deny an inmate's use of it.

I believe that many inmates are impoverished and would lack resources to purchase pot. It is a relatively cheap substance, easily grown I am told.

d) There may be state laws prohibiting people from smoking tobacco in indoor public places. Such laws seemed to be promised on the fact that second-hand smoke bothers some people. Even if that were true an all-out ban is too broad, unduly interfering with the smoker's property and right to pursue happiness. If offended, the non-smoker can usually go elsewhere. It should be easy to insulate the non-smoker bothered by the smoke.

e) I don't think that the moderate use of alcohol in a prison or jail is out of line. If one gets out of hand, he can be excluded from future sessions. All this, like tobacco, at government expenses. Alcohol use in a tightly regulated setting can easily be monitored. If there is an occasional brawl, corrections personnel should be able to handle it.

Perhaps even the chronic drunk driver, if conditioned to drink in moderation, may carry over upon discharges.

f) I spent 4 months 4 times at the Norfolk Regional Center in the late 80s and 90s. While I'm pretty sure that the food fell within federal guidelines, I never looked forward to eating a meal as none was ever tasty. The facility now houses a sex offender program. I haven't heard whether the food has improved.

I've been at many others mental health centers and most had good enough food. From my perspective, the quality of the food is of utmost importance, with the psychiatric treatment expected to be by one who is incompetent.

I've recently sampled food at the Madison County (NE) jail and the food is atrocious.

g) Music soothes the soul, I have it on when I go to sleep.

h) One of Jesus' requirements was to visit the imprisoned. I take this injunction seriously. I've been told by an inmate in the Nebraska penal system that it takes months to arrange for visitation. In my case, transportation is a problem.

It is my understanding that all penal institutions require one to state in advance who he intends to visit. Since I know so few, I would want to visit inmates at random. Of course, if none wanted to visit it would be a wasted trip.

38. The testimony of two or three witnesses is necessary to establish a crime. Deuteronomy 19:15 THE JERUSALEM BIBLE.

39. The government must have a compelling interest to interfere with a fundamental right. Regulations of legitimate rights must be strictly drawn, *Roe v. Wade*, 410 U.S. 113, 155 (1973).

40. If the plaintiff has suffered no harm, the defendant shouldn't be punished. "For the end of government being the preservation of all, as such as may be, even the guilty are to be spared, where it can prove no prejudice to the innocent, John Locke's, *Treatise on Government*, second Essay XIV § 159.

41. Principles # 7, 8 and 9 above shall be applied retroactively in the court systems.

V

The World Religions, in denial of the Bible, are false but not blameworthy simply because of not having the bible.

2.   In one or more respects, religions purporting to follow Jesus are false religions simply because they fall short of adhering to all Jesus' commands.

3.   The claim being made here is that only The God of Daniel religion is a True religion, True to the Bible in all respects.

4.   Roman Catholicism in all likelihood is the most corrupt religion on the planet, as will be explained.

5.   Fervent Catholics take such pride in holding that since it has existed since the time of Jesus Christ, it must be the best and truest religion.

6.   That it is one, holy, Catholic and apostolic church is in every sense a misnomer. It is not one because there is a plethora of Jesus-inspired religions. It is not holy: witness the crusades and the inquisition. It is not Catholic because it is not universal; it is Roman. It is not apostolic as it cannot demonstrate that the apostles were the founding fathers. The Acts of the Apostles, while

giving sparse attention to Peter and John focuses on Paul, the self-proclaimed 13th Apostle.

7. Jesus lived in simplicity and poverty.

8. By contrast, the Roman Catholic Church is opulent and a many splendored thing, while the present pope lives in meagre surroundings, he is surrounded by riches.

9. As to policy or moral guidance, the church plays fast and loose with Jesus' teachings.

10. Any religion, to be true, must be true in all respects. Jesus never charged a penny for his teachings.

Bread and wine
Consider Matthew

[Matthew 26:26-29]

[26] And as they were eating, Jesus took bread, and blessed it, and brake it, and gave it to the disciples, and said, take, eat; this is my body.

[27] And he took the cup, and gave thanks, and gave it to them, saying, drink ye all of it;

[28] For this is my blood of the new testament, which is shed for many for the remission of sins.

[29] But I say unto you, I will not drink henceforth of this fruit of the vine, until that day when I drink it new with you in my Father's kingdom.

and Mark

[Mark 14:22-25]

22 And as they did eat, Jesus took bread, and blessed, and brake it, and gave to them, and said, take, eat: this is my body.

23 And he took the cup, and when he had given thanks, he gave it to them: and they all drank of it.

24 And he said unto them, this is my blood of the new testament, which is shed for many.

25 Verily I say unto you, I will drink no more of the fruit of the vine, until that day that I drink it new in the kingdom of God.

11. It should be noted that neither of these two stated that the Eucharist was to be repeated. Compare [Luke 22:19-22] in which text there is a command to repeat the process.

[Luke 22: 19-22]

19 And he took bread, and gave thanks, and brake it, and gave unto them, saying, this is my body which is given for you: this do in remembrance of me.

20 Likewise also the cup after supper, saying, this cup is the new testament in my blood, which is shed for you.

21 But, behold, the hand of him that betrayeth me is with me on the table.

22 And truly the Son of man goeth, as it was determined: but woe unto that man by whom he is betrayed!

12. Thirty years ago I read a Bible in English which was a Dutch version. It had a footnote to the effect that many early Bibles did not have the admonition to do this in memory of me. Bruce Metzger, *a Textual Commentary on the Greek New Testament* indicates that there is a longer and a shorter text but didn't quote either.

13. Consequently, the testimony of two men, Matthew and Mark, is true and the Lukan account is bogus. So the Catholic Church has historically snubbed Matthew and Mark. The Catholic Church ignores the controversy.

War

14. "There will be wars and rumors of wars, let that not alarm you." Yet all recent popes have ignored these words, perpetually engaged in peace talks and making public statements calling for world peace.

15. The popes recklessly make void the words of Jesus.

16. **On the rest of Christianity**

17. I don't know of a single Christ-based religion that does not celebrate the bread and wine. None practice what the Bible teaches in that regards.

On the World Religions

18. As stated earlier, those outside the Bible influence will be saved easily. Ignorance is our excuse.

On Atheism and other non-believers

19. Atheists assert that no one has proved the existence of God. They are also correct in holding that there is not one True religion. The emergence of the God of Daniel religion may destroy both perceptions. But I can't count on persuading all non-believers that God exists.

At this point I'll briefly assess weaknesses of individual religions.

a)   The Jews

20. It is widely believed that Moses is the founder of Judaism, if so, it is not the testimony of two men, so may be discredited on this basis.

21. The Old Testament is filled with covenants between God and the Jews. In my view, among the most significant was Leviticus 26:3-13.

[Leviticus 26:3-13]

³ If ye walk in my statutes, and keep my commandments, and do them;

⁴ Then I will give you rain in due season, and the land shall yield her increase, and the trees of the field shall yield their fruit.

⁵ And your threshing shall reach unto the vintage, and the vintage shall reach unto the sowing time: and ye shall eat your bread to the full, and dwell in your land safely.

⁶ And I will give peace in the land, and ye shall lie down, and none shall make you afraid: and I will rid evil beasts out of the land, neither shall the sword go through your land.

⁷ And ye shall chase your enemies, and shall fall before you by the sword.

⁸ And five of you shall chase a hundred, and a hundred of you shall put ten thousand to flight: and your enemies shall fall before you by the sword.

⁹ For I will have respect unto you, and make you fruitful, and multiply you, and establish my covenant with you.

¹⁰ And ye shall eat old store, and bring forth the old because of the new.

[11] And I will set my tabernacle among you: and my soul shall not abhor you.

[12] And I will walk among you, and will be your God, and ye shall be my people.

[13] I am the Lord your God, which brought you forth out of the land of Egypt, that ye should not be their bondmen; and I have broken the bands of your yoke, and made you go upright.

22. God promised peace and prosperity if they would faithfully observe his commandments.

If they failed many bad things would occur.

[Leviticus 26:14-39]

[14] But if ye will not hearken unto me, and will not do all these commandments;

[15] And if ye shall despise my statutes, or if your soul abhor any judgments, so that ye will not do all my commandments, *but* that ye break my covenant:

[16] I also will do this unto you; I will even appoint over you terror, consumption, and the burning ague, that shall consume the eyes, and cause sorrow of heart: and ye shall sow your seed in vain, for your enimies shall eat it.

[17] And I will set my face against you, and ye shall be slain before your enemies: they that hate you shall reign over you; and ye shall flee when none persueth you.

[18] And if ye will not yet for all this hearken unto me, then I will punish you seven times more for your sins.

[19] And I will break the pride of your power; and I will make your heaven as iron and your earth as brass:

²⁰ And your strength shall be spent in vain: for your land shall not yield her increase, neither shall the trees of the land yield their fruits.

²¹ And if ye walk contrary unto me, and will not hearken unto me; I will bring seven times more plagues upon you according to your sins.

²² I will also send wild beasts among you, which shall rob you of your children, and destroy your cattle, and make you few in number; and your *high* ways shall be desolate.

²³ And if ye will not be reformed by me by these things, but will walk contrary unto me;

²⁴ Then will I also walk contrary unto you, and will punish you yet seven times for your sins.

²⁵ And I will bring a sword upon you, that shall avenge the quarrel of my covenant: and when ye are gathered together within your cities, I will send the pestilence among you; and ye shall be delivered into the hand of the enemy.

²⁶ And when I have broken the staff of your bread, ten women shall bake your bread in one oven, and they shall deliver you your bread again by weight: and ye shall eat, and not be satisfied.

²⁷ And if ye will not for all this hearken unto me, but walk contrary unto me;

²⁸ Then I will walk contrary unto you also in fury; and I, even I, will chastise you seven times for your sins.

²⁹ And ye shall eat the flesh of your sons, and the flesh of your daughters shall ye eat.

³⁰ And I will destroy your high places, and cut down your images, and cast your carcases upon the carcases of your idols, and my son shall abhor you.

³¹ And I will make your cities waste, and bring your sanctuaries unto desolation, and I will not smell the savour sweet odours.

[32] And I will bring the land into desolation: and your enemies which dwell therein shall be stonished at it.

[33] And I will scatter you among the heathen, and will draw out a sword after you: and your land shall be desolate, and your cities waste.

[34] Then shall the land enjoy her Sabbaths, as long as it lieth desolate, and ye be in your enemies' land; even then shall the land rest, and enjoy her Sabbaths.

[35] As long as it lieth desolate it shall rest; because it did not rest in your Sabbaths, when ye dwelt upon it.

[36] And upon them that are left alive of you I will send a faintness into their hearts in the lands of their enemies; and the sound of a shaken leaf shall chase them; and they shall flee, as fleeing from a sword; and they shall fall when none pursueth.

[37] And they shall fall one upon another, as it were before a sword, when none pursueth: and ye shall have no power to stand before your enemies.

[38] And ye shall perish among the heathen, and the land of your enemies shall eat you up.

[39] And they that are left of you shall pine away in their iniquity in your enemies' lands; and also in the inquities of their fathers shall they pine away with them.

23. Even if they then made amends for their iniquities God would renew his covenants with Jacob, Isaac and Abraham.

[Leviticus 26:40-45]

[40] If they shall confess their iniquity, and the iniquity of their fathers, with their trespass which they trespassed against me, and that also they have walked contrary unto me:

⁴¹ And that I also have walked contrary unto them, and have brought them into the land of their enemies; if then their uncircumcised hearts be humbled, and they then accept of the punishment of their iniquity:

⁴² Then will I remember my covenant with Jacob, and also my covenant with Isaac, and also my covenant with Abraham will I remember; and I will remember the land.

⁴³ The land also shall be left of them, and shall enjoy her Sabbaths, while she lieth desolate without them: and they shall accept of the punishment of their iniquity: because, even because they despised my judgments, and because their soul abhorred my statutes.

⁴⁴ And yet for all that, when they be in the land of their enemies, I will not cast them away, neither will I abhor them to destroy them utterly, and to break my covenant with them: for I am the Lord their God.

⁴⁵ But I will for their sakes remember the covenant of their ancestors, whom I brought forth out of the land of Egypt in the sight of the heathen, that I might be their God: I *am* the Lord.

24. While Jesus was popular for a time, eventually religious leaders convinced the people to turn against him as they chose for release the infamous Barabbas over Him. See Matthew 27:17, 20.

[Matthew 27:17–20]

¹⁷ Therefore when they were gathered together, Pilate said unto them, whom will ye that I release unto you? Barab'bas, or Jesus which is called Christ?

¹⁸ For he knew that for envy they had delivered him.

¹⁹ When he was set down on the judgment seat, his wife sent unto him, saying, have thou nothing to do with that

just man: for I have suffered many things this day in a dream because of him.

²⁰ But the chief priests and elders persuaded the multitude that they should ask Ba-rab'bas, and destroy Jesus.

25. The last straw was when the Jews took total responsibility for Jesus' crucifixion:

[Matthew 27:24-25]

²⁴ When Pilate saw that he could prevail nothing, but that rather a tumult was made, he took water, and washed his hands before the multitude, saying, I am innocent of the blood of this just person: see ye to it.

²⁵ Then answered all the people, and said, his blood be on us, and on our children.

26. And the Jews have been cursed ever since.

b) Protestants

27. In being correct in assessing Roman Catholicism as corrupt, they can be faulted for not forming a single, true-in-all-respects religion. Protesting isn't enough to establish a religion that is 100% in accord with the gospels. Total reformation was in order.

c) Church of Jesus Christ Latter Day Saints.

28. History shows that Joseph Smith formed the religion so that his is not the testimony of two men; Brigham Young came later.

29. According to one commentator, Steven Mansfield. *The Mormonizing of America* (Worthy Publishing; Brentwood TN) the following are among the features of Mormonism: 1) emphasis on

family; 2) high value on education. *Id.* Matthew 11:25; 3) the sacred duty of service (to the government); 4) being high achievers. (arguably if talented they shouldn't waste their talents).

30. On the surface they have two features that seem to be Jesus-inspired. They have 12 apostles and they send out missionaries 2x2. These are only superficialities. It seems as though they appoint the oldest 12 men they can find as apostles, as is frequently reported in the media. The first 4 chosen – Peter, Andrew, James and John were fishermen working for their fathers so it is highly likely that they were not old, so selecting someone in an advanced state to name apostle makes no biblical sense. Consider the following:

[Luke 10:1-16]

[1] After these things the Lord appointed other seventy also, and sent them two and two before his face into every city and place, whither he himself would come.

[2] Therefore said he unto them, the harvest truly *is* great, but the labourers are few: pray ye therefore the Lord of the harvest, that he would send forth labourers into his harvest.

[3] Go your ways: behold, I send you forth as lambs among wolves.

[4] Carry neither purse, nor scrip, nor shoes, and salute no man by the way.

[5] And into whatsoever house ye enter, first say, peace *be* to this house.

[6] And if the son of peace be there, your peace shall rest upon it: if not, it shall turn to you again.

[7] And in the same house remain, eating and drinking such thins as they give: for the labourer is worthy of his hire. Go not from house to house.

[8] And into whatsoever city ye enter, and they receive you, eat such things as are set before you:

⁹ And heal the sick that are therein, and say unto them, the kingdom of God is come nigh unto you.

¹⁰ But into whatsoever city ye enter, and they receive you not, go your ways out into the streets of the same, and say,

¹¹ Even the very dust of your city, which cleaveth on us, we do wipe off against you: notwithstanding be ye sure of this, that the kingdom of God is come nigh unto you.

¹² But I say unto you, that it shall be more tolerable in that day for Sodom, than for that city.

¹³ Woe unto thee, Cho-ra'zin! Woe unto thee, Beth-sa'i-da! For if the mighty works had been done in Typre and Si'don, which have been done in you, they had a great while ago repented, sitting in sackclosth and ashes.

¹⁴ But it shall be more tolerable for Tyre and Si'don at the judgement, than for you.

¹⁵ And thou, Ca-per'-na-um, which art exalted to heaven, shalt be thrust down to hell.

¹⁶ He that heareth you heareth me; and he that despiseth you despiseth me; and he that despiseth me despiseth him that sent me.

31. In the 80s I had first-hand experience with some missionaries. They lived in their own apartment and received a monthly stipend not at all like Luke 10.

d) Jehovah's Witnesses

32. Prominent features of this religion seem to be a distrust of government and based upon which I perceive to be an obscure passage in the Old Testament, an abhorrence of blood transfusion. My first encounter with the Witnesses in which I was the first to inform them that I had doubts about the validity of Paul.

33. Their AID TO BIBLE UNDERSTANDING, left on my door step, proved to be a very valuable resource.

34. They later came down with a 2-volume set, INSIGHT INTO THE SCRIPTURES, which I didn't really like as well.

35. It is a fair statement that I wouldn't be at this point in my biblical awareness without the guidance of the Jehovah's Witnesses. The AID TO BIBLE UNDERSTANDING is an achievement that should find its way into the hands of every serious student of the Bible. I've often stated: "Truth is where you find it."

    e)   Native Americans

36. From my limited knowledge all I can say is that some of the tribes espoused "peace" while having war capabilities. I may be wrong, but I think they were capable of war even before the white man arrived.

    f)   Islam

37. I started reading the Koran years ago, but found it more difficult to read the further I got into the text. As I recall, there was some reference to Jesus and Mary from a source called Evangel (which I haven't seen). Muhammad considered Jesus a great prophet, but not the son of God. Needless to say, the religion has no belief in the trinity.

38. There is ample support in the Koran for what is called fundamentalism (Terrorism, or cutting off the heads of infidels who refused to convert to the religion is clearly sanctioned). While they have undertaken to convert the world to Islam by force, I have hopes that by making them aware of the God of Daniel religion, they will recognize that truth overshadows brute force.

VI

Jesus was a humble preacher, and not easily given to anger. But he was apparently very upset about the money-changers in the temple:

[John 2:13-22]

¹³ And the Jews' Passover was at hand, and Jesus went up to Jerusalem.

¹⁴ And found in the temple those that sold oxen and sheep and doves, and the changers of money sitting:

¹⁵ And when he had made a scourge of small cords, he drove them all out of the temple, and the sheep, and the oxen; and poured out the changers' money, and overthrew the tables;

¹⁶ And said unto them that sold doves, take these things hence; make not my Father's house a house of merchandise.

¹⁷ And his disciples remembered that it was written, the zeal of thine house hath eaten me up.

¹⁸ Then answered the Jews and said unto him, what sign shewest thou unto us, seeing that thou doest these things?

¹⁹ Jesus answered and said unto them, destroy this temple, and in three days I will raise it up.

²⁰ Then said the Jews, forty and six years was this temple in building, and wilt thou rear it up in three days?

²¹ But he spake of the temple of his body.

²² When therefore he was risen from the dead, his disciples remembered that he had said this unto them; and

they believed the scripture, and the word with Jesus had said.

2. His disdain of Pharisees permeated the gospels, see, e.g.

[Mark 7:1-3]

¹ Then came together unto him the Pharisees, and certain of the scribes, which came from Jerusalem.

² And when they saw some of his desciples eat bread with defiled, that is to say, with unwashen, hands, they found fault.

³ For the Pharisees, and all the Jews, except they wash *their* hands oft, eat not, holding the tradition of the elders.

The key word above is tradition. All of Mark 7 and Matthew 15 focus on a stern denunciation of tradition which is man-made commands and not the Word of God, the two chapters are nearly identical as will be shown shortly the Catholic church, in its own words, thrives on its tradition shutting out the Word of God.

All of chapter 23 of Matthew presents as riveting indictment: scattered throughout the gospels were examples of how the Pharisees were attempting to trick Jesus. All of Matthew 23 was a constant rebuke of the Pharisees. The reader is urged to examine Mark 7, Matthew 15 and 23. They will be repeated in the next part.

3. Paul was trained as a Pharisee and never abandoned that status:

[Acts 23:6]

6 But when Paul perceived that the one part were Sad'du-cees, and the other Pharisees, he cried out in the council, men *and*

brethren, I *am* a Pharisee, the son of a Pharisee: of the hope and resurrection of the dead I am called in question.

4. Consequently, Paul's epistles must be considered works not in keeping with Jesus' sayings; this means that all subsequent theologians, pastors, preachers etc, who do not recognize what Paul says as an outcast rather than legitimate spokesman for Jesus, are themselves Pharisees. If his words are those of a Pharisee, they cannot and should not be deemed the Word of God.

5. The book called Acts of the Apostles is a misnomer, reciting very little about the genuine 12 and dwelling on the self-proclaimed 13th apostle. While the book deals with Peter to some extent, what is not generally appreciated is that he was not a good apostle of Jesus: compare the following versus from Mark.

[Mark 8:38]

38 Whosoever therefore shall be ashamed of me and of my words in this adulterous and sinful generation; of him also shall the Son of man be ashamed, when he cometh in the glory of his Father with the holy angels.

[Mark 14:66-72]

66 And as Peter was beneath in the palace, there cometh one of the maids of the highest priest:

67 And when she saw Peter warming himself, she looked upon him, and said, and thou also wast with Jesus of Nazareth.

68 But he denied, saying, I know not, neither undertand I what thou sayest. And he went out into the porch; and the cock crew.

⁶⁹ And a maid saw him again, and began to say to them that stood by, this is one of them.

⁷⁰ And he denied it again. And a little after, they that stood by said again to Peter, surely thou art one of them: for thou art a Galilean, and thy speech agreeth thereto.

⁷¹ But he began to curse and to swear, saying, I know not this man of whom ye speak.

⁷² And the second time the cock crew. And Peter called to mind the word that Jesus said unto him, before the cock crow twice, thou shalt deny me thrice. And when he thought thereon, he wept.

6. I claim that by these words Peter abandoned his claim to salvation and status as an apostle.

7. Missing is the story of the real apostles. What did they do after Jesus ascended into heaven?

8. I submit that no one knows. There exists only speculation. See C. Bernard Ruffin, *The Twelve* (Our Sunday Visitor: Huntington in June 1984).

9. I further submit that it is *possible* that they are alive and well and waiting for a sign from heaven. After all some of the early individuals mentioned in Genesis lived long, e.g. Adam lived for 932 years. Genesis 5:5.

10. "The first shall be last and the last shall be first." As far as I know these words have never been interpreted. I'm claiming that they refer to myself. Peter is the first apostle shall be last and I am the last that apostle that shall be first. It may seem bold and outlandish, but I believe my interpretation to be correct.

11. What is the meaning of the following passage?

[Matthew 21:18-22]

¹⁸ Now in the morning as he returned into the city, he hungered.

¹⁹ And when he saw a fig tree in the way, he came to it, and found nothing thereon, but leaves only, and said unto it, let no fruit grow on thee henceforward for ever. And presently the fig tree withered away.

²⁰ And when the disciples saw it, they marveled, saying, how soon the fig tree withered away!

²¹ Jesus answered and said unto them, verily I say unto you, if ye have faith, and doubt not, ye shall not only do this which is done to the fig tree, but also if ye shall say unto this mountain, be thou removed, and be thou cast into the sea; it shall be done.

²² And all things, whatsoever ye shall ask in prayer, believing, ye shall receive.

12. I would submit that at that time the apostles had little faith and *did not doubt at all* they would cast a mountain into the sea. This, of course, hasn't happened yet.

13. There is a presumption in my mind that the remaining books in the New Testament are frivolous, or partly as they will have to be examined paragraph by paragraph.

14. It was the man-made rules of the Pharisees that earned Jesus' sharp rebuke of them from time to time. Tradition is severely criticized in Mark 7 and Matthew 15, as noted above.

15. Under the general heading THE TRANSMISSION OF DIVINE REVELATION from paragraphs 75 through 97 of the *Catechism of the Catholic Church* (1999) the authors boast of one form or another of tradition in the Catholic Church without a single

reference to Mark 7 and Matthew 15. It scored a whopping 19 times.

16. What follows is a list of topics encompassed by the Catechism, but for which there is no gospel support for:

Recorded

1066	Liturgy
1233	Baptism without immersion as John the Baptist did
1877	Human community
1950	When Jesus used the word mourn
1928	Social justice
734	Justification
2030	Church, Mother of Theodor
2102	Vows
2104	Religious freedoms
2177	Sunday Holy day
2204	The Christian Family
2207	The family and society
2270	Abortions
2276	Euthanasia's
2307	Avoiding Wars
2354	Pornography
2350	Homosexuality
2389	Sexual abuse of young
2419	Social Doctrine of Church
2426	Economic activity and social justice
2437	Justice and solidarity among nations
675	Antichrist
2496	Use of social communications media
2502	Sacred art

2634	Prayer of Intercession
2637	Prayer of Thanksgiving
2673	Prayer with Holy Mother of God
2683	Prayer: a cloud of witnesses
2691	Places favorable for prayer
2709	Contemplative prayer
2734	Filial trust
2743	Persevering in love
2352	Masturbation
3288	Respect for health

17. The cites for the above are derived from epistles or later Christian writers but no gospel sources.

Just take the first item liturgy. The Mass, Benediction, and so on are not derived from Jesus. All others will be discussed in part 2.

18. The icing on the cake is the church's "indispensable minimum" to attain salvation (footnotes, none of which cite to my gospel omitted.)

THE PRECEPTS OF THE CHURCH

2041   The precepts of the church are set in the context of a moral life bound to and nourished by liturgical life. The obligatory character of these positive laws decreed of the pastoral authorities is meant to guarantee to the faithful in indispensable minimum in the spirit of prayer and moral effort, in the growth in love of God and neighbor.

2042   The first precept ("You shall attend Mass on Sundays and holy days of obligation") requires the faithful to participate in the Eucharistic celebration when the Christian community gathers together on the day commemorating the Resurrection of the Lord the second precept ("You shall confess your sins at least once a year,") ensures preparation for the Eucharist by the reception of the sacrament of reconciliations which continues baptism's work of conversion and forgiveness.

The third precept ("you shall humbly receive your creator in Holy Communion at least during the Easter season,") guarantees as a minimum the reception of the Lord's Body and Blood in connection with the paschal feasts, the origin and center of the Christian liturgy.

2043   The fourth precept ("you shall keep holy the holy days of obligation") completes the Sunday services by participating in the principal liturgical feasts which honor the mysteries of the Lord, the Virgin Mary, and the saints.

The fifth precept ("you shall observe the prescribed days of fasting and abstinence.") Ensures the times of penance which prepare us for the liturgical feasts; they help us acquire mastery over our instincts and freedom of heart.

[The six precept] "The faithful also have the duties of providing for the material needs of the church, each according to his abilities."

19. Not one precept from Jesus, the church is hopelessly and stupidly stupid *in tradition,* man-made rules, the church is "making void the word of God through your tradition that you have handed down." quoted in Mark 7:13.

Isaiah has rightly prophesized about the hypocrites leading the church:

[Mark 7:6-7]

⁶ He answered and said unto them, well hath E-sai'as prophesied of you hypocrites, as it is written, this people honoureth me with their lips, but their heart is far from me.

⁷ Howbeit in vain do they worship me, teaching for doctrines the commandments of men.

VII

Anyone attempting to speak or preach the gospel on behalf of Jesus has a dual burden.

2. One attempting to preach the gospel and not recognizing the shortcomings of Paul as himself or herself a bully in all likelihood. They have forfeited the right to speak on Jesus' behalf.

3. Any Christian pastor, duped by Paul, is without standing to preach about God and is unfit for ministry.

4. There is no record that Jesus ever charged for his teachings.

[Matthew 22:15-22]

¹⁵ Then went the Pharisees, and took counsel how they might entangle him in *his* talk.

¹⁶ And they sent out unto him their disciples with the He-ro'di-ans, saying, master, we know that thou art true, and teachest the way of God is truth, neither carest thou for any *man*: for thou regardest not the person of men.

¹⁷ Tell us therefore, what thinkest thou? Is it lawful to give tribute unto Caesar, or not?

¹⁸ But Jesus perceived their wickedness, and said, why tempt ye me, ye hypocrites?

¹⁹ Shew me the tribute money. And they brought unto him a penny.

²⁰ And he saith unto them, whose is this image and superscription?

²¹ They say unto him, Caesar's. Then saith he unto them, render therefore unto Caesar the things which are Caesar's; and unto God the things that are God's.

²² When they had heard these words, they marvelled, and left him, and went their way.

5. What is significant is that Jesus said: Show me a coin, so logically, he had none.

Consider also:

[Matthew 17:24-27]

²⁴ And when they were come to Ca-per'na-um, they that received tribute money came to Peter, and said, doth not your master pay tribute?

²⁵ He saith, yes. And when he was come into the house, Jesus prevented him, saying, what thinkest thou, Simon? Of whom do the kings of the earth take custom or tribute? Of their own children, or of strangers?

²⁶ Peter saith unto him, of strangers. Jesus saith unto him, then are the children free.

²⁷ Notwithstanding, lest we should offend them, go thou to the sea, and cast a hook, and take up the fish that first cometh up; and when thou hast opened his mouth, thou shalt find a piece of money: that take, and give unto them for me and thee.

Once again Jesus is without funds.

6. The message for today's preachers is that they must neither ask for nor accept money for preaching, as there is not a hint in the gospels that Jesus had my earnings.

7. The preachers may howl. How are we to preach the gospel? This is precisely the point as they are neither fit nor qualified to preach for Jesus.

8. TV Ministries

9. With their never ending plea to sell books and tapes and otherwise extract money from the gullible, they talk the talk (bullshit) as they are not men of God prepared to expose false religion to any government so they can't walk the walk (they are stepping in the bull shit).

10. I will write a couple of examples: Billy Graham and the Billy Graham Ministries. He has gone solo for years, which means the testimony of another witness is missing. The emergence of his son Franklin doesn't pick up the slack. I don't really know if the son does television like the father, but I see him on TV sometimes during the Christmas season touting his silk purse campaign (possibly it is son's purse of something else). This organization sends shoe boxes full of goodies to children around the world. I'm reasonably sure that funds don't come from secret donations, nor am I inclined to state: "Well done, servant, as you are giving charity secretly."

11. Another favorite is Pat Robertson's 700 Club. I don't think he calls this club a ministry, but the seeking of money is a key component. He continually speaks (I think prays – with his eyes closed? – "in Jesus' name." Whether or not a religion, I'm sure it has tax-exempt status).

12. I'm sure the legal status of non-profit never existed at the time Jesus lived. I'm equally sure that were he to come down from the clouds and walk on earth, he would not rush to file a 501(c), if I have it right. You can bet your house that the God of Daniel Religion will never join the ranks of the legal non-profits. (I'm curious, will the federal bureaucrats recognize my religion as being a genuine religion without the non-profit tag?)

13. Although I don't watch, it seems as though son Gordon Robertson is a replacement for the elder founder. As with "the Reverend Mr. Graham," "The Reverend Pat Robertson" founded his club without the assistance of anyone else: One witness. When I was hospitalized recently I couldn't help but identify myself as a Reverend Mr. Graham Cracker.

14. There are far too many television ministries for me to discuss individually in this book. But I can't leave without a mention of Jimmy Swaggart: is he more pleasing to God because he is more versatile: playing the piano, singing, crying. Has any preacher picked up the soft shoe?

15. I will end on a serious note: Larry Ankenbauer. In the 80s I used to thoroughly enjoy his half-hour shows on cable on Sunday mornings. His approach was to invite 2 "experts" with apparently opposing views, and to question each to find out the truth of his issue. I'm unable to pinpoint how many time he succeeded, if at all. For if these "experts" truly spoke for God, it would be a valuable half hour. In any event, I give Mr. Ankenbauer an "A" for effort as in each program he was searching for the truth.

16. Recently, I happened to see him again, having aged, but he was doing the same thing, so, in not claiming to know the truth about God himself, but in seeking it out, he is one of God's winners. I hope to meet him someday. I believe that he, too, sells tapes and/

or books to finance his show. I would hope that he could hook up with an independent source of funding or limit his sales to occasions in which his questioning did lead to some aspect of truth (Possibly he has never hit pay dirt).

17. Better yet, I would hope that he could convince the cable outlet to absorb the costs of production, advertising that he is the only worthwhile television ministry.

18. I can't rest without mentioning the late Fulton J. Sheen who enjoyed pretty good ratings success on primetime TV for a few years. Then I was in high school.

19. He had a ridiculous cape. (was that Catholic monsignor garb at the time?) He always wrote something on the blackboard. His words were unscripted. He always told at least one joke. I kept watching, even though I never understood anything he was saying, he used what I would call big words.

20. Nevertheless, I was inspired by the title of the program: "Life is Worth Living" as he was so upbeat. I always assumed that he knew what he was talking about. But since his vocabulary was beyond my comprehension, his message for the specific programs never got through to me.

21. If I ever watch repeats, perhaps I can judge him soundly. Was he merely the Howard Cossell of religion?

VIII

BEL AND THE DRAGON[a]

Daniel and the priests

14 [b]When King Astyages joined his ancestors, Cyrus of Persia succeeded him. Daniel was very close to the king, who respected him more than any of his other friends.[c] •Now, in Babylon there was an idol called Bel,[d] to which twelve bushels of the finest flour, forty sheep and six measures of wine were offered every day. •The king venerated this idol and used to go and worship it every day. Daniel, however, worshipped his own God. •'Why do you not worship Bel?' the king asked Daniel. 'I do not worship idols made by human hand,' Daniel replied, 'I worship the living God who made heaven and earth and who is lord over all living creatures.' 'Do you not believe, then,' said the king, 'that Bel is a living god? Can you not see how much he eats and drinks each day?' •Daniel laughed. 'Your Majesty,' he said, 'do not be taken in; he is clay inside, and bronze outside, and has never eaten or drunk anything.' •This made the king angry; he summoned his priests, 'Tell me who eats all this food,' he said, 'or die.'ᵉ Prove to me that Bel really eats it, and I will have Daniel put to death for blaspheming him.' •Daniel said to the king, 'Let it be as you say.'

There were seventy of these priests, to say nothing of their wives and children. The king went to the temple of Bel, taking Daniel with him.ᶠ The priests of Bel said to him, 'We shall now go out, and you, Your Majesty, will lay out the meal and mix the wine and set it out. Then, lock the door and seal it with your personal seal. If, when you return in the morning, you do not find that everything has been taken by Bel, let us be put to death; otherwise let Daniel, that slanderer!' •They were thinking––hence their confidence––of a secret entrance which they had made under the table, and by which they came in regularly and took the offerings away. When the priests had gone and the king had set out the food for Bel, •Daniel made his servants bring ashes and spread them all over the temple floor, with no other witness than the king. They then left the building, shut the door and, sealing it with the king's seal, went away. •That night, as usual, the priests came with their wives and children; they ate and drank everything.

The king was up very early next morning, and Daniel with him. •'Daniel,' said the king, 'are the seals intact?' 'They are intact, Your Majesty,' he replied. •The king then opened the door and, taking one look at the table, exclaimed, 'You are great, O Bel! There is no deception in you!' •But Daniel laughed; and, restraining the king from going in any further, he said, 'Look at the floor and take note whose footmarks these are!' •'I can see the footmarks of men, of women and of children,' said the king, •and angrily ordered the priests to be arrested, with their wives and a children. They then showed him the secret door through which they used to come and take what was on the table. •The king had them put to death and handed Bel over to Daniel who destroyed both the idol and its temple.

Daniel kills the dragon

There was a great dragon which the Babylonians worshipped too.[g] •The king said to Daniel, 'Are you going to tell me that this is made of bronze? Look, it is alive; it eats and drinks; you cannot deny that this is a living god; worship it, then.' •Daniel replied, 'I will worship the Lord my God; he is the living God. With your permission, Your Majesty, without using either sword or club, I shall kill this dragon.' 'You have my permission,' said the king. •Whereupon, Daniel took some pitch, some fat and some hair and boiled them up together, rolled the mixture into balls and fed them to the dragon; the dragon swallowed them and burst. Daniel said, 'Now look at the sort of thing you worship!'. •The Babylonians were furious when they heard about this and rose against the king. 'The king has turned Jew,' they said, 'he has allowed Bel to be overthrown, and the dragon to be killed, and he has put the priests to death.' •So they went to the king and said, 'Hand Daniel over to us or else we shall kill you and your family.' •They pressed him so hard that the king found himself forced to hand Daniel over to them.

Daniel in the lion pit[h]

They threw Daniel into the lion pit, and there he stayed for six days. •In the pit were seven lions, which were given two human bodies and two sheep every day; but for this period they were not given anything, to make sure they would eat Daniel.

Now, the prophet Habakkuk was in Judaea: he had been making a stew and breaking up bread into a basket. He was on his way to the fields, taking this to the harvesters, •when the angel of the Lord spoke to him, 'Take the meal you are carrying to Babylon, and give it to Daniel in the lion pit,' •'Lord,' replied Habakkuk, 'I have not even seen Babylon and know nothing about this pit.' •The angel of the Lord took hold of his head and carried him off by the hair to Babylon where, with a great blast of his breath, he set Habakkuk down on the edge of the pit. 'Daniel, Daniel,' Habakkuk shouted, 'take the meal that God has sent you.' And Daniel said, 'You have kept me in mind, O God; you have not deserted those who love you.' •Rising to his feet, he ate the meal, while the angel of God carried Habakkuk back in a moment to his own country.

On the seventh day, the king came to lament over Daniel; on reaching the pit he looked inside, and there sat Daniel. •'You are great, O Lord, God of Daniel,' he exclaimed, 'there is no god but you!' •He then had Daniel released from the pit and the plotters of Daniel's ruin were thrown in instead, where they were instantly eaten before his eyes.

THE JERUSALEM BIBLE (footnotes omitted.)

I must have read this chapter at least 50 times before I came upon what I deem to be the definitive explanation: If one is truly a man of God, he'll be able to identify and expose false religion to the government. I reached this conclusion in April 1987.

X

Religion should foster the enjoyment of life, liberty, health, property and the pursuit of happiness as well as equal rights for all.

2. Government has no end but to protect these rights.

3. Government must have a compelling interest to interfere with fundamental rights.

    a) an allegation of violation of fundamental rights must be raised.

    b) an appropriate tribunal should be designated to adjudicate these rights.

    c) an appeal may or may not be allowed.

4. Rights of less than a constitutional dimension shall be adjudicated as set forth in par. 3 above.

XI

Sports are a fundamental part of life.

2. The undersized plans to publish a short book with a change of rules of some sports.

3. Society should transition toward sports Thursday through Monday (extended days of the Sabbath – personal view of author not directed by God).

XII

It is intended that this religion be world-wide.

2. As such, this book is to be distributed only in English.

3. All foreign countries are encouraged to adapt the United States Constitution.

4. The God of Daniel Religion has no church structure, so there exists no reason to ever build a church again.

5. Jesus taught in Judea and Galilee. He traveled by foot all the time, it would seem. It is clear that he never sought (nor did he receive) compensation of any sort.

6. I'm on social security. Consequently, financial constraints require that I charge for the sale of this book! Were I not to choose this course of action I would get very few books circulated. Of course, I don't anticipate world wide acceptance overnight.

7. In 21st century America Jesus might be able to spread the word for free by the media (which didn't exist when he walked the earth) if they followed Him. Today I can't connect free TV and radio.

8. For practical reasons the God of Daniel Religion can't match Jesus' penury. Jesus preached and taught in Jerusalem and surrounding areas, all within walking distance.

9. The God of Daniel Religion, obviously not destined to be confined to a small geographic area, must compromise in hopes of reaching a world-wide audience and so charges for the purchase of this book. Except perhaps for the Gideons, no one is giving Bibles away. The Gideons are many.

10. I anticipate that there will be no additional efforts by this religion to fleece society (except for future volumes).

11. Selectivity. Inasmuch as some of the content of this religion is new, even radical, one is allowed to pick and choose which portions he or she will embrace. It is hoped that over time, it will be embraced totally.

XIII

October 15, 2015

I thought I had put this book to bed. Then I met Daniel Kleve, a 20-yr-old student who told me that he was a Satanist and that he had utter disdain for Christianity, the biggest culprit being the Catholic Church. Despite his tender years, he had devoured a host of sources over a 5-year period to reach his shockingly novel "to me" position that Satan meant truth and that Jehovah was a deceiver, a myth, the same as Jesus.

2. I abandoned Catholicism years ago when I abruptly discovered that their leaders from early history were corrupt. I had always known that they were untrustworthy for the reason that they took great pride in suppressing ideas that they didn't like.

3. I have learned conclusively, I believe, that much of the Old Testament is in the category of "something borrowed" from other religions, which Satanists decry as something stolen.

4. The God of Daniel Religion accepts the core Jesus as the gospel truth, and that no other religion by policy and practice is biblically acceptable.

5. Read Article Jesus The Stone Builder, spiritual Alchemy, and YHUH New Kingdom.

Jesus said: "On this rock I will build my church...." This means he was only planning on one church and that the many thousands of Christians churches can not constitute one church.

6. The Acts of the Apostles does not chronicle what the 12 chief disciples did. Rather they are mainly centered upon Paul's activities. Self-proclaimed as the 13th apostle – if Jesus Paul's wanted 13, doesn't it follow that he would have had 13 at the time he lived?

7. Jesus said: "I am the Way, the Truth and the Life" no reason exists to believe that He believed this bold statement to be partially true, that he would rely on someone later to modify or add to the Truth. The many examples of Tradition found in the Catechism of the Catholic Church, listed earlier, can be linked to the presumptuousness of Paul.

8. What did the original 12 do after Jesus left earth? NO ONE KNOWS.

9. The God of Daniel Religion's working hypothesis is that the 12, except for the unceremonious Peter, have not been yet fully trained and prepared to spread the gospel throughout the world yet.

10. In other words, Catholic and Christian faiths are bogus. Paul, a blathering idiot, took on the role of being Jesus' chief spokesman without a knowledge and understanding of what Jesus said.

11. All Christians have tricked themselves into the bread and wine ceremony repetition, a man-made tradition as explained earlier. None advocate and promote secret prayer as clearly ordered by Jesus. Almsgiving is to be secret, according to Jesus; by almsgiving to the poor or disadvantaged would seem to be key and a church is not a proper recipient. In this regard all the churches' reliance

upon donations from the flock is obviously counter to the way Jesus spread his message. Jesus had no need of a collection plate.

12. Insofar as every Christian religion fails to follow simple but clear messages of Jesus, each is disqualified from claiming to be "My Church."

13. I would cite two more examples: 1) Jesus said that if the disciples had sufficient faith they'd be able to cast a mountain into the sea.

14. I happen to believe that miracles can happen and that Jesus wasn't whistling Dixie when He made that statement. 2) Refer to the Parable of the Sower, quoted and discussed below: The seed is sown, for various reasons, only some of it sprouts and grows; in the end it matures. This is how I interpret Jesus' precious words. Maturation didn't occur 2000 years ago, only with the creation of the God of Daniel Religion, officially founded in 1987.

15. In 1987 the God of Daniel Religion began with two tenets: "False religions were unacceptable," and that if one is truly a man of God he'll be able to identify and expose false religion to the government, Truth, no one would dispute, is the opposite of false. By truth, then undefined, I think that I meant scientific and (I suppose that includes mathematics) and Biblical Truth. But that year I thought that my recognition of the importance of truth was a significant achievement. It was my thought at the time that being in truth was not a prerequisite for any of the many Christian religions.

16. At the time I wondered who would identify and expose. These two principles are deprived from Daniel 13 and 14, found only in Catholic and Mormon bibles. There are no indicators whatsoever that either of these religions has adopted this interpretation, so there is no "man of God" on the horizon in either the Roman Catholic

or the Church of Jesus Christ of Latter-day Saints. Since the rest of Christianity does not acknowledge these texts, they have no biblical basis for assuming such a role.

17. By 2015 I have decided that it is my fate to be the man of God mentioned above. Although there is much planning to be done, I believe that somehow I have the burden of going forward with governments —— and I mean world-wide governments —— making the God of Daniel Religion all done as a world-wide religion.

18. If a religion fails to follow the clear messages of Jesus the religion has no right to be called His Church. I would go further: Jesus is commonly known as the Christ. Christ means Messiah or liberator. But, if the truth be told, Jesus has not liberated anyone – neither Jew nor Gentile – and thus can't be called the Messiah. Consequently, the God of Daniel Religion is not a Christian religion, but a biblically-based, a Jesus-based one. I can't say that the religion is in accord hook, line and sinker simply because I have not mastered in every respect the Gospels. Many claim they believe everything in the Bible, but I don't think anyone could come close to having full comprehension.

19. At this point the God of Daniel Religion is at a crossroads. In reliance upon truth as being my ultimate goal, I remember what I have always told myself in recent years: "Truth is where you find it." (I don't recall whether I read this quote somewhere or whether I just figured it out.)

20. I have believed for many years that truth is the Word of God, as Jesus said. Until January 1984 I believed that Catholicism was the repository of truth. That abruptly changed in early 1984 when intense reading of 3 bibles hastened me to abandon Catholicism forever.

21. The emergence of Satanism into my mindset 2 months ago or so meant there now exists a competition for truth. For one following the Bible, Satan is the great deceiver. For a Satanist, Satan is Truth, the God of the Old Testament doesn't exist; Jesus didn't exist in history and was a myth.

22. My dilemma: Truth or consequences. As Pontius Pilate was said to have asked: "What is Truth?"

23. The Satanists have scads and scads of resources, many of which are findable on the internet. If I pose a question to my friend (a member of the Joy of Satan – JoS), he may refer me to from one to ten sources. The first was a volume nearly 600 pages. Mercifully there have been many short articles which I found helpful.

24. With respect to the subject, I want to tread lightly and not misinterpret the religion I have decided to submit this division to sum for a summary of the essence of His religion.

25. Satanism predates the old testament of centuries. Their leaders point out that most of the O.T. has been stolen from other religions. Jesus, too, is said to be an example from many prior religions. For example, many religions have had their own version of death on a cross or tree. There is precedent for birth by a virgin by other religions.

26. The claim is made that many of Jesus' sayings stem from other religions and that He says nothing original, or statements that are contradictory.

27. The biggest complaint is that Jesus didn't exist in history but is only a fictional character.

28. One quote that caught my attention: "Nazareth did not exist in the 1st century AD – the area was a burial ground of rock-cut tombs." Kenneth Humphreys

29. If this be true, a Christian source should have discovered and reported it years ago. If Humphrey wanted to be pissy, he could have conjectured that Jesus was the original Barney Rubble. Score one for the Satanists over the "Christians." The God of Daniel Religion believes the religion "experts" on the bible have egg on their face in this regard, but this is a trifling matter. What is important is His words and actions.

30. Ponder a statement from "Literary Traditions: Ten Reasons the Gospels are Works of Fiction" a skeptics blog on May 02, 2011: "Furthermore, Paul's message was distinctly not Jesus' message. Paul preached a different message, and more than this, he changed the message of Christ to be his own." This remark is not small potatoes. It is in accord with my independent observations reported earlier. Paul, the "good Pharisee being blind," has been uncritically followed by all after him. I might say that if Jesus were in His grave, he might be turning over, but he is not in his grave and, being all-knowing, was fully aware that the course of "Christianity" would ensure (falsely in His name).

In conclusion – "A surplus of evidence shows the bulk of the Bible's Content is a historical, discrepancy filled, incongruent, inharmonious, and has been embroidered and embellished upon time and again...." The ten reasons and this conclusion merit full consideration which will be done in the next volume.

13 Catholicism has from the beginning been entrenched in suppression of ideas, meaning that the leaders have had no regard for the truth. For many centuries they have been very cruel to those who failed to toe the line.

Satanists are very concerned with the truth. There is no history whatsoever of them burning books. I've seen no evidence of violence on their part; to the contrary, I have read that they are opposed to it.

31. Harking back to the Carpenters: "We've only just begun" to explore the writings of the Satanists. The early readings put Catholicism and Christianity to shame. The Satanists seem to be honorable, good thinkers. I'm reasonably certain that a follower has a right to reject ideas proposed if he has a view that differs.

32. While they have seen fit to reject the Bible and more specifically Jesus, it is my hope at this time they can embrace at least tentatively. The God of Daniel Religion as presenting a welcome aberration to the Bible. From my brief introduction to the JoS I can continue to explore their religion. As noted above, I've got to pay attention to all critics be the Satanists, atheists, others even of a Christian bent — any logical thinker.

33. At this point I will make a brief assessment of my God of Daniel religion. Prior to October 1, 2015 I was smugly content with the religion's content, it having extracted the highlights of the Old Testament and the gospels. Of course, it is impossible to discuss every issue the Bible might throw at you — the shorter the religions book the better. As long as I convinced myself I was on a path of the "best of," I could pick and choose what I thought comprised the best. Anyone disagreeing is free to reject any or all of it, start his own religion or maintain the status quo as a Christian, whatever that means.

34. My introduction to Satanism was a book called *Exposing Christianity*, which I found to be disjointed and filled with repetitions. The terminology employed left me more baffled than enlightened. It was hardly a literary masterpiece. (I should talk. All

my writings fall short of ideal and would undoubtedly be improved were I to hire a competent editor).

35. The exposure of Old Testament material having been documented as stolen was eye-opening. The historical domination of Jewery over Christianity was emphasized, but there were insufficient details to have me convinced. Finally, and most important, specific gospel sayings were quoted and disparaged. I thought this segment was both superficial and weak. At this point I don't choose to battle over each quote of Jesus that was maligned.

36. First impressions don't have to be lasting impressions. As my friend fed me other sources, mostly articles, (but also books that I have yet to delve into) this newly discovered religion seems to make more and more sense. While *Expressing Christianity* left me dumbfounded, (I made copious notes which I forwarded to my friend for clarification, it hasn't happened yet), the initial research has me wanting more.

37. A self-assessment following my exposure to the Joy of Satan publications means that I am no longer in the smug category. For example, the traditional (Biblical) view of Satan has been undermined, probably even for the better. Jehovah's "truth" and Satan's "truth" are at odds. (The careful reader will note that the word Satan has been implied to be something evil in my writings).

38. Although I am unable to quote the exact verse at this time, Jesus said in effect, "The Father and I are One." Surely he didn't mean Father Satan.

39. There will probably be a need for a future updated text on the God of Daniel Religion. Time will only tell whether the Joy of Satan and this Biblically inspired religion can be reconciled.

40. I really hate to say it, but it is *possible* that upon further inquiry I may be forced to substitute the God of Daniel Religion as bullshit, just as I did Catholicism. "Truth is wherever you find it."

41. In this respect, I recall the famous TV star of yesteryear, a comedienne named Lily Tomlin. She was famous for monologues. In some of them she would babble on for some time and then realize that she had dug herself into an intellectual hole and she would end it all by saying: "Never Mind." I hope I don't reach the juncture where I have to say this is bullshit or never mind. "The end," would be a satisfactory ending.

42. I, of course, reserve the right to examine Satanism with a critical eye. While the early return is that Job is legitimately clinging to truth as a goal, in their own minds, the same can certainly not be said for Catholicism and Christianity. The belated recognition of Satanism reaffirms my disposition in 1984 to immediately bolt from Catholicism, undeniably steeped in "lying eyes." The Eagles.

The end – for now

XIV

November 15, 2015

Five years ago or so I conjured up in my mind the beginning of a plan for world peace. Obviously one cannot realistically say that today is the day of peace. An announcement of a plan is surely not enough. There must be implementation.

2. Of course, the announcement of my plan at that time would have been foolhardy. It is neither overstatement or understatement to recognize that I was then a veritable pipsqueak. Hopefully, with this and my other late 2016 writings my voice may have some weight.

3. During the winter of 2016 and 2017 I may have gained considerable stature. Since I have unveiled a third testament to the Bible in this volume —— something no one in the world could possibly have anticipated —— yet I think that this introduction is a well-founded success. Others may disagree, but I think that all "experts" submerged in Christianity blindly following Paul are in no position to refute me. One and all lack credibility for failing to explore the nature of, if any, and the extent to which, if any, Paul is a reliable spokesman for Jesus. Outsiders have done him in. I am an outsider because from my earliest encounter I was not sold on Paul as I informed the Jehovah's Witnesses in 1984. But at that time my status was obviously one of being a neophyte in biblical understanding and interpretation. As is often stated, it is sometimes

good to think outside the box, were I a Paulene rubber stamp I never would have toppled him.

4. If *ROE v. WADE* is Unconstitutional as Justice Blackmun Lied also proves to be an influential destruction of the case on its own terms as written by Blackmun's own words, this may be another feather in my literary cap. When this book hits the landscape I fully anticipate that the number of abortions performed per year will plummet from 1,000,000+ to 1,000-. There is a chance that the figure would be higher than the thousand, but I am without accurate statistics to make a specific prediction.

5. Completing the publishing trifecta in my winter of contentment is BUCKING POWER: Bad Law and New Order SVU (?) in which a hodge-podge of laws will be declared unconstitutional by the courts. If I am correct there will be societal revolutions here and there. I am not out to gain instant popularity by many of my unprecedented proposals, but my raising the issues for the first time, is merely my own opinion that I, having studied the constitution more than anyone else, am qualified to provide ammunition for attorneys to challenge the status quo. If my own conclusions fail to sway courts here and there, I won't lose any sleep –– at least for that reason.

6. Self-proclaiming #1 status as happiest person in the world is promised on my belief that I am closer to God than any other human at the present time. Writing three great –– again, my opinion – or gangbusters books, more or less simultaneously, only explodes my feelings of happiness.

7. My most recent stay in Faith Regional Center may indicate to the nurses and techs that I was on the downside of life because I yelled a lot. I had super reasons for my frequent outbursts. I enjoyed complaining to high heaven because the "Treatment Team" put

it in my treatment plan that I couldn't have hot food when two microwave ovens were nearby to reheat food that had become room temperature as it was transported 2 to 3 miles from another building. Second, while it was necessary for me to contact 3 to 5 attorneys pertaining to various court proceedings, the "Team" selected the most incompetent and unethical as the only one I could contact –– and he refused to talk to me. I was effectively denied access to courts. Letters, correspondence, concerns even about daily matters were to be forwarded to a guardian-brother at Emerson Nebraska. The whole process might take up to 21 days; he had the option to throw them away. I had other complaints which I will not go into at this time.

8. All in all, I am at peace of mind, a prerequisite, I think, to realistically being in a position to change the war-torn landscape of the world.

9. My plan begins in Syria, but I'll provide no details at this time, which requires the cooperation and assistance of others. Central will be exposing false religion.

10. A peace pipe can be delayed a year or so.

11. In closing this chapter, I am ever mindful of Jesus' words that whoever exalts himself shall be humbled and he who humbles himself shall be exalted. I hope that my self-indulging in this chapter is only temporary but necessary to elevate myself to the status of world peace-maker.

XV

For years the title of this volume was fixed as The God of Daniel Religion. However, as I was finishing the work, I concluded that the more encompassing THE THIRD TESTAMENT, part I was more appropriate, with the original relegated to the secondary.

2.   The meaning of the biblical text has been improved upon here as nowhere else in several particulars.

3.   First of all, *Abortion and the Outlaw* published in 1989 with little distribution made the observation that a religion must be true to be acceptable to God. The Protestant Revolution may definitely be seen as an improvement in that a corrupt Catholicism was rejected, yet none established a religion comporting with Jesus' requirements.

4.   The same volume indicated that only a true man of God could identify and expose false religion to the government.

5.   The above are interpretations of Daniel 13 and 14 found only in Catholic and Mormon bibles, so that the rest of Christendom is lacking in biblical guidance and the Catholics and Mormons have not seized on these interpretations. For either of them to attempt to argue as I have, they would have to reject their entire heritage.

6.   The prophet Gideon required absolute proof before he would undertake to serve God as a leader. This author is claiming to be a

modern Gideon and that absolute proof is not a priority – multiple clues are sufficient.

7.   A significant achievement of Jesus in biblical –– religions –– interpretation is that the testimony of two men is true. This undoubtedly will be helpful in weeding out the false and contradictory statements attributed to Jesus in TTT part 2. To what extent are the words in the gospels authentic? What if anything can be salvaged from the remainder of the new testament? Hopefully these issues can be resolved in part 2.

8.   An example of how this works: Buddhism is the testimony of one man, Buddha, Hinduism, with no certainty of origin, is obviously not the testimony of 2 men.

9.   Jesus said that the first shall be last but the last first. I have never seen such an interpretation. I'm claiming that Peter was the first apostles and that I am the last. Who is to refute me?

10. The Parable of the Sower is obviously of great importance as it appears verbatim in all 4 gospels. My interpretation is that only after a great deal of time does the good seed mature. I am claiming that the good seed is now in the process of ripening.

[Matthew: 13:1-23]

¹ The same day went Jesus out of the house, and sat by the sea side.

² And great multitudes were gathered together unto him, so that he went into a ship, and sat; and the whole multitude stood on the shore.

³ And he spake many things unto them in parables, saying, behold, a sower went forth to sow;

⁴ And when he sowed, some seeds fell by the way side, and the fowls came and devoured them up:

⁵ Some fell upon stony places, where they had not much earth: and forthwith they sprung up, because they had no deepness of earth.

⁶ And when the sun was up, they were scorched; and because they had no root, they withered away.

⁷ And some fell among thorns; and the thorns sprung up and choked them:

⁸ But other fell into good ground, and brought fort fruit, some a hundredfold, some sixtyfold, some thirtyfold.

⁹ Who hath ears to hear, let him hear.

¹⁰ And the disciples came, and said unto him, why speakest thou unto them in parables?

¹¹ He answered and said unto them, because it is given unto you to know the mysteries of the kingdom of heaven, but to them it is not given.

¹² For whosoever hath, to him shall be given, and he shall have more abundance: but whosoever hath not, from him shall be taken away even that he hath.

¹³ Therefore speak I to them in parables: because they seeing see not; and hearing they hear not, neither do they understand.

¹⁴ And in them is fulfilled the prophecy of E-sai'as, which saith, by hearing ye shall hear, and shall not understand; and seeing ye shall see, and shall not perceive:

¹⁵ For this people's heart is waxed gross, and *their* ears dull of hearing, and their eyes they have closed; lest at any time they should see with *their* eyes, and hear with their ears, and should understand with their heart, and should be converted, and I should heal them.

¹⁶ But blessed are your eyes, for they see: and your ears, for they hear.

[17] For verily I say unto you, that many prophets and righteous men have desired to see those things which ye see, and have not seen them; and to hear those things which ye hear, and have not heard them.

[18] Hear ye therefore the Parable of the Sower.

[19] When any one heareth the word of the kingdom, and understandeth it not, then then cometh the wicked one, and and catcheth away that which was sown in his heart. This is he which received seed by the way side.

[20] But he that received the seed into stony places, the same is he that heareth the word, and anon with joy recieveth it;

[21] Yet hath he not root in himself, but dureth for a while: for when tribulation or persecution ariseth because of the word, by and by he is offended.

[22] He also that received seed among the thorns is he that heareth the word; and the care of this world, and the deceitfulness of riches, choke the word, and he becometh unfruitful.

[23] But he that received seed into the good ground is he that heareth the word, and understanndeth it; which also beareth fruit, and bringeth forth, some a hundredfold, some sixty, some thirty.

11. Were it not for my understanding of this parable and the emergence of my religion I would not have dared to have attached the word TESTAMENT to this volume.

12. Jesus made a strong denunciation of Pharisees, Paul claimed *to be* a good Pharisee not that he *was* a good Pharisee. All Christian leaders (and laity) following have failed to realize that we must be wary of the Pharisee Paul and his writings.

13. I have identified and sketched several clues in this short volume that cry out for discernment. No one else has bothered to realize that there should in all likelihood be a repository demonstrating that what Jesus said is true that's why the need for an additional testament.

14. My understanding of this parable is the primary reason that I advance the claim of status of being God's number one spokesman at this time.

15. This beginning poses a challenge to anyone claiming to speak on behalf of Jesus I hope. A long time ago I read, but I'm not certain where any longer, that both Peter and Paul expected a second coming of Jesus sooner rather than later. Had they, or anyone since, captured the Parable of the Sower, they might have had a legitimate claim to be God's number one servant. If I am correct in my assertion it will be difficult to unseat me; but if it of God's will I have no objection.

16. In the next volume I will elaborate on many issues raised here if there exists feedback requesting it. If I made any errors I would want to set the record straight.

17. A conclusion that must be emphasized: Jesus' wrath was against the Pharisees, the leaders. My rancor rests on them as well and I have not a slight problem with the Laity who have been duped all of these centuries.

Printed in the United States
By Bookmasters